DEEPAK CHOPRA

with Kristina Tracy

ON MY WAY

TO A HAPPY LIFE

illustrated by

Rosemary Woods

Library of Congress Control Number: 2009927977

ISBN: 978-1-4019-2575-8
Digital ISBN: 978-1-4019-2946-6

17 16 15 14   7 6 5 4
1st edition, November 2010
4th edition, January 2014

Printed in Shenzhen, China, by Bookplus
Files submitted to printer: July 1, 2010

 HAY HOUSE, INC.
Carlsbad, California • New York City
London • Sydney • Johannesburg
Vancouver • Hong Kong • New Delhi

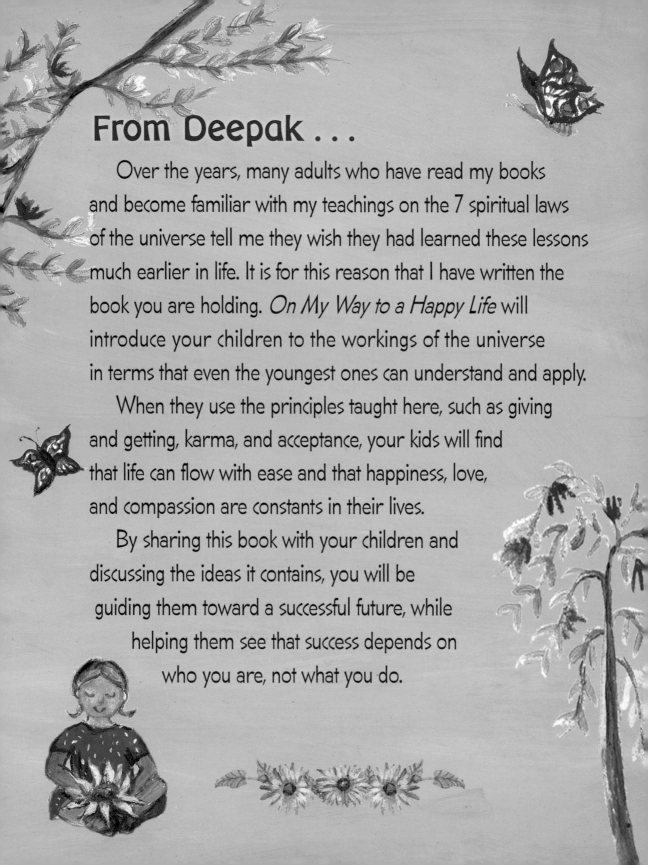

From Deepak . . .

Over the years, many adults who have read my books
and become familiar with my teachings on the 7 spiritual laws
of the universe tell me they wish they had learned these lessons
much earlier in life. It is for this reason that I have written the
book you are holding. *On My Way to a Happy Life* will
introduce your children to the workings of the universe
in terms that even the youngest ones can understand and apply.

When they use the principles taught here, such as giving
and getting, karma, and acceptance, your kids will find
that life can flow with ease and that happiness, love,
and compassion are constants in their lives.

By sharing this book with your children and
discussing the ideas it contains, you will be
guiding them toward a successful future, while
helping them see that success depends on
who you are, not what you do.

Anything Is Possible

There's something
incredible inside of you.
It's the power
to make all your
dreams come true.

The gift you've been given is that you can create
absolutely anything, whether small or great.

So imagine, believe, and
set your dreams free.

There is no limit to what
you can do or be.

Way to a Happy Life ～

BELIEVE THAT
ANYTHING IS POSSIBLE

Giving and Getting

Do you want more friends, more fun,
more of just . . . whatever?

There's an easy way to get it—
it really is quite clever.

Give the things you want to get
every single day

and you will find the very same things
coming back your way.

Always give with a happy heart—
that's what makes it real.

The greatest gift of all is (surprise!)
just how good you'll feel.

Way to a Happy Life ～
GIVE WHAT YOU WANT TO GET

What You Do Comes Back to You

Karma is an ancient word
you may hear people say.

It means that how
you live your life creates
what comes your way.

Every day you decide the things you say and do, and what you choose will change the way others act toward you.

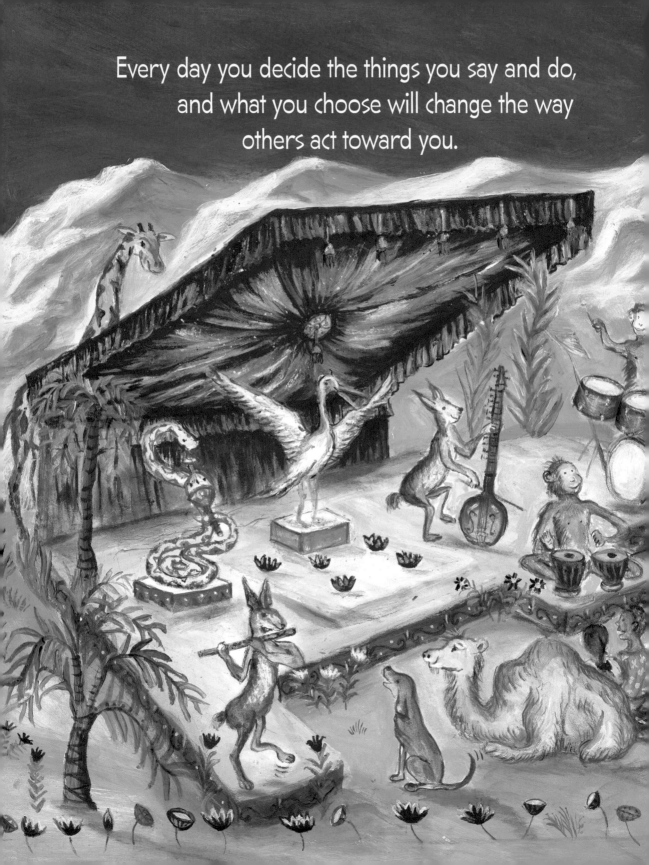

Your heart will gladly guide you in the choices that you make,
and your karma will follow you—good luck is no mistake!

Way to a Happy Life ~

FOLLOW YOUR HEART—
IT KNOWS WHAT TO DO

Creating Peace

Sometimes you may wish that
things were different
than they are.

But when you learn acceptance,
life will be easier by far.

You won't always understand what other people do,
but know that change can happen when it starts with you.

Trying to control the world . . . well, it just can't be done.
You alone can create peace—your place in the sun.

Way to a Happy Life ~
CREATE PEACE
BY LEARNING ACCEPTANCE

Growing What You Want

If you want
something to happen,
then do these simple things.
Set your mind on what
you wish for, then see
what the future brings.

Do the work, plant the seed,
and believe that it will grow.
After you have done these things,
it's time to just let go.

In your heart you can be sure
that nature will do the rest.
The universe has a plan for you
and will always do what's best.

Way to a Happy Life ～

WORK TOWARD WHAT YOU WANT, THEN LET IT GO

Be Open to Life

Sometimes it feels like
life's a maze and you don't
know what's in store.

Always be ready to turn down
a path you may not
have taken before.

If you think there's only one way that something can be done,
learning that there are many ways makes life a lot more fun!

The more you are open to new ideas of how your life can be,
the more happiness you will have—try it and you'll see.

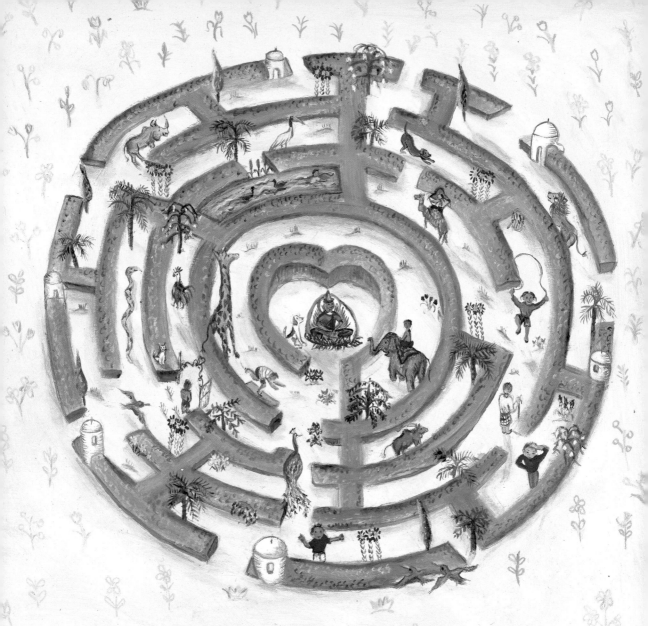

Way to a Happy Life ~

BE OPEN TO
NEW WAYS AND IDEAS

Your Place in the World

Your dharma is your
purpose, it's why
you're here on Earth.

It's a gift that you
were given in
the time before your birth.

You have a special talent that is unique to you.
When you're doing this one thing,
your happiness feels true.

If you don't know what your dharma is—
don't worry, you'll find out.
It may be soon or not for years, but you
will know it without a doubt.

You'll share your dharma with many, or with just a few.
It doesn't matter as long as you share it—
that's why it was given to you.

Way to a Happy Life ~

FIND YOUR DHARMA
AND FIND BLISS (HAPPINESS)

You have now learned the ways of nature
and the universe—the way that things always
have and always will work. When you
understand these ideas and use them in
your life, you will flow with nature,
and life will be full of joy!

— Deepak Chopra

We hope you enjoyed this Hay House book.
If you'd like to receive our online catalog featuring additional information on
Hay House books and products, or if you'd like to find out more about the
Hay Foundation, please contact:

Hay House, Inc.
P.O. Box 5100
Carlsbad, CA 92018-5100

(760) 431-7695 or **(800) 654-5126**
(760) 431-6948 (fax) or **(800) 650-5115 (fax)**
www.hayhouse.com® • **www.hayfoundation.org**

Published and distributed in Australia by: Hay House Australia Pty. Ltd., 18/36 Ralph St.,
Alexandria NSW 2015 • Phone: 612-9669-4299 • Fax: 612-9669-4144 • www.hayhouse.com.au

Published and distributed in the United Kingdom by: Hay House UK, Ltd., Astley House, 33 Notting Hill
Gate, London W11 3JQ • Phone: 44-20-3675-2450 • Fax: 44-20-3675-2451 • www.hayhouse.co.uk

Published and distributed in the Republic of South Africa by: Hay House SA (Pty), Ltd., P.O. Box 990,
Witkoppen 2068 • Phone/Fax: 27-11-467-8904 • www.hayhouse.co.za

Published in India by: Hay House Publishers India, Muskaan Complex, Plot No. 3, B-2, Vasant Kunj,
New Delhi 110 070 • Phone: 91-11-4176-1620 • Fax: 91-11-4176-1630 • www.hayhouse.co.in

Distributed in Canada by: Raincoast Books, 2440 Viking Way, Richmond, B.C. V6V 1N2 •
Phone: 1-800-663-5714 • Fax: 1-800-565-3770 • www.raincoast.com

Take Your Soul on a Vacation

Visit **www.HealYourLife.com®** to regroup, recharge, and reconnect with your own magnificence.
Featuring blogs, mind-body-spirit news, and life-changing wisdom from Louise Hay and friends.

Visit **www.HealYourLife.com** today!